STEM IN THE SUMMER OLYMPICS
THE SCIENCE BEHIND
TENNIS

by Jenny Fretland VanVoorst

CANCEL

Ideas for Parents and Teachers

Pogo Books let children practice reading informational text while introducing them to nonfiction features such as headings, labels, sidebars, maps, and diagrams, as well as a table of contents, glossary, and index.

Carefully leveled text with a strong photo match offers early fluent readers the support they need to succeed.

Before Reading

• "Walk" through the book and point out the various nonfiction features. Ask the student what purpose each feature serves.

• Look at the glossary together. Read and discuss the words.

Read the Book

• Have the child read the book independently.

• Invite him or her to list questions that arise from reading.

After Reading

• Discuss the child's questions. Talk about how he or she might find answers to those questions.

• Prompt the child to think more. Ask: Different tennis courts affect the speed with which the ball moves. Have you ever played tennis? What was the court made of? Was it a fast or slow court?

Pogo Books are published by Jump!
5357 Penn Avenue South
Minneapolis, MN 55419
www.jumplibrary.com

Library of Congress Cataloging-in-Publication Data

Names: Fretland VanVoorst, Jenny, 1972- author.
Title: The science behind tennis / by Jenny Fretland VanVoorst.
Description: Minneapolis, MN: Pogo Books, published by Jump!, Inc., [2020]
Series: STEM in the Summer Olympics
Includes bibliographical references and index.
Audience: 7 to 10.
Identifiers: LCCN 2019001170 (print)
LCCN 2019003036 (ebook)
ISBN 9781641289108 (ebook)
ISBN 9781641289085 (hardcover: alk. paper)
Subjects: LCSH: Tennis—Juvenile literature. | Sports sciences—Juvenile literature.
Classification: LCC GV996.5 (ebook) | LCC GV996.5 .F74 2020 (print) | DDC 796.342—dc23
LC record available at https://lccn.loc.gov/2019001170

Editor: Susanne Bushman
Designer: Michelle Sonnek

Photo Credits: optimarc/Shutterstock, cover (clipboard); ID1974/Shutterstock, cover (racquet); DuxX/Shutterstock, cover (ball); A.RICARDO/Shutterstock, 1; Elnur/Shutterstock, 3; 506 collection/Alamy, 4; Aflo Co. Ltd./Alamy, 5; PA Images/Alamy, 6-7; Leonard Zhukovsky/Shutterstock, 8-9, 18-19; Alex Ionas/Shutterstock, 10 (top); Alhovik/Shutterstock, 10 (bottom); Jorgeprz/Shutterstock, 11; Xinhua/Alamy, 12-13; Guzel Studio/Shutterstock, 14 (foreground); Jatuporn Sawatmuang/Shutterstock, 14 (background); SvedOliver/Shutterstock, 15; Luis Acosta/AFP/Getty, 16-17; SewCream/Shutterstock, 20-21; Africa Studio/Shutterstock, 23.

Printed in the United States of America at Corporate Graphics in North Mankato, Minnesota.

TABLE OF CONTENTS

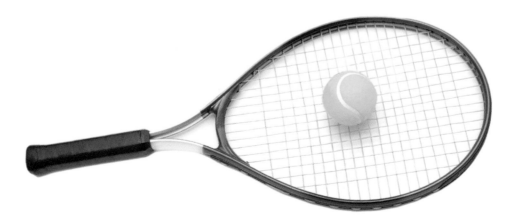

CHAPTER 1

MAKING A RACQUET

Pow! Balls fly. Racquets swing. Tennis is fast-paced. It is exciting. It can also be a science lesson.

racquet

An Olympic tennis player relies on a racquet. It is used to create a powerful **stroke**. The ball hits the racquet's strings. It flies off!

Tennis racquets should be stiff. Why? When Olympians hit the ball, the racquet frame **vibrates**. This absorbs the ball's **energy**. The ball slows down. A stiffer frame vibrates less. It absorbs less energy. The ball keeps more energy. It can fly faster and farther.

TAKE A LOOK!

Where the ball hits the strings is important. Take a look!

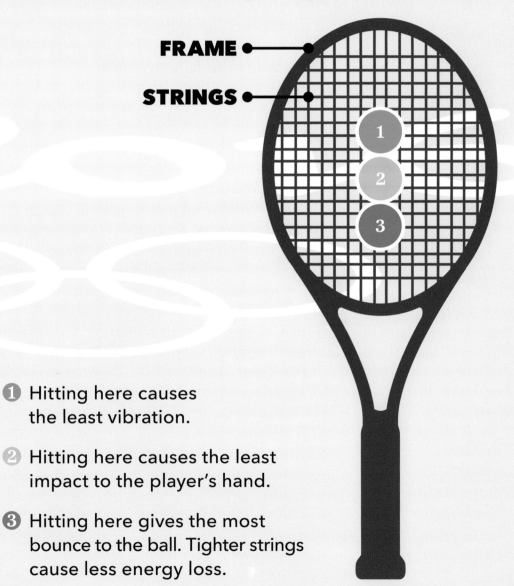

FRAME

STRINGS

1 Hitting here causes the least vibration.

2 Hitting here causes the least impact to the player's hand.

3 Hitting here gives the most bounce to the ball. Tighter strings cause less energy loss.

Strings help, too. How? When a ball hits the strings, they stretch. They store some of the ball's **kinetic energy**. They quickly return the energy back to the ball. This is called the snap-back effect. The more the strings stretch, the more power they store and give back.

CHAPTER 2

EYE ON THE BALL

The tennis ball soars. Air slows it down. This is called **drag**.

Large, fluffier tennis balls have more drag. More drag means a slower flight. This gives the other player more time to prepare.

Gravity plays on the ball, too. Players use this force to help their game. How? They hit with **topspin**. This creates a downward force and a shorter shot. **Backspin** has the opposite result. It creates an upward force. It allows the ball to sail long. These strokes enhance or lessen the force of gravity.

CHAPTER 3

ON THE COURT

Slam! The ball hits the court. Drag is replaced by **friction**.

clay court

A rough surface means greater friction. Like what? Clay courts. These are called slow courts. The ball loses speed on its bounce.

Other courts create less friction. The ball loses less speed on grass courts. These are called fast courts.

What do they use in the Olympics? Hard courts. These are asphalt or concrete. The surface is neither slow nor fast. But it does not **cushion** player's feet.

DID YOU KNOW?

Courts become faster the longer they are used. Why? Use smooths the surface.

JOHNSON Steve

USA   15
0

GBR   40
0

MURRAY Andy

CHALLENGES REMAINING   TIME 0:03
JOHNSON Steve   3
MURRAY Andy   3

139

Rio2016 Rio2016

hard court

Tennis players run and jump. Their feet apply force to the court. An equal and opposite force acts on the player. This is a **reaction force**. It can cause injury. Special shoes cushion the players' feet. They reduce the effect of the reaction force.

DID YOU KNOW?

Tennis was first played at the Olympics in 1896. At first, only men played. Women could compete starting in 1908.

Olympians know the science behind tennis. They use it to take home gold. Can you use science to win big?

ACTIVITIES & TOOLS

BOUNCE SCIENCE

See how friction affects the speed and height of a tennis ball's bounce with this activity!

What You Need:
- a tennis ball
- a friend
- measuring tape
- a variety of flat surfaces, such as concrete, carpet, grass, linoleum, tile, and hardwood

❶ Choose your starting surface. Make sure the area is flat and even.

❷ Hold the tennis ball in your hand and extend your arm straight out in front of your body, parallel to the floor or ground. Drop the ball without applying force.

❸ Ask your friend to use the measuring tape to measure the height at which the ball bounces. Record the data.

❹ Repeat the exercise two more times. Record your results.

❺ Move to another surface and repeat three more times. Continue until you run out of surfaces to try.

❻ Now look at your data. How did the different surfaces affect the ball's bounce? On which surface did the ball bounce the highest?

GLOSSARY

backspin: A stroke that causes the ball to rotate backward after it is hit, creating an upward force.

cushion: To reduce the force of an impact.

drag: The force that slows or blocks motion or advancement.

energy: The ability of something to do work.

force: An action that produces, stops, or changes the shape of a movement or object.

friction: The force that slows down objects when they rub against each other.

gravity: The force that pulls objects toward the center of Earth and keeps them from floating away.

kinetic energy: The energy of motion.

reaction force: An equal force that is applied in the opposite direction of impact.

serves: Begins play by throwing the ball into the air and hitting it with the racquet.

stroke: A hit or swing.

topspin: A stroke that causes the ball to rotate forward after it is hit, creating a downward force.

vibrates: Moves back and forth or from side to side rapidly to produce a quivering effect.

INDEX

TO LEARN MORE

Finding more information is as easy as 1, 2, 3.

❶ **Go to www.factsurfer.com**

❷ **Enter "sciencebehindtennis" into the search box.**

❸ **Choose your book to see a list of websites.**

FACT SURFER